Advance Reader Copy
For Promotional Use Only

World Poetry Books
Pub Date: November 12, 2026

Publicity Contact:
publicity@worldpoetrybooks.com

Ordering and Distribution Info:
worldpoetrybooks.com/orders
orders@worldpoetrybooks.com

Ernst Herbeck

In His One Languages

Selected Poems

translated from German by
David Brazil and Gary Sullivan

WORLD POETRY

Ernst Herbeck
In His One Languages: Selected Poems

First Edition, First Printing, 2026
ISBN 978-1-954218-52-9

World Poetry Books
New York, NY
www.worldpoetrybooks.com

World Poetry titles are distributed by Asterism Books (US) and Turnaround Publisher Services (UK). Subscriptions and standing orders are available from the publisher.

Library of Congress Control Number: 2026948903

Cover design by Clever Hans
Typesetting by Don't Look Now
Printed in Lithuania by BALTO Print

The translation of this book was supported by the Deutscher Übersetzerfonds (German Translators' Fund) and the Bundesministeriums für Wohnen, Kunst, Kultur, Medien und Sport (Federal Ministry of Housing, Arts, Culture, Media and Sport).

World Poetry Books is a 501(c)(3) nonprofit and charitable organization founded in 2017 in New York City, a member of the Community of Literary Magazines and Presses (CLMP), and a member of the publishing cooperative Poetry Corp. Our publications and programs are made possible by grants from the Poetry Foundation, Hawthornden Foundation, and the New York State Council on the Arts with the support of the Office of the Governor and the New York State Legislature, and supported by an affiliation with the Humanities Institute and the Translation Program at the University of Connecticut (Storrs), as well as individual donors and subscribers. To learn more or to make a donation please visit our website: worldpoetrybooks.com/support.

Federal Ministry
Housing, Arts, Culture,
Media and Sport
Republic of Austria

Table of Contents

Introduction

Ernst Herbeck was born in Stockerau, Austria, in 1920, the same year as Paul Celan.

This is not an idle observation.

Both poets created significant and influential bodies of literature that bear the scars of extreme cultural, generational, and personal trauma. Both grappled with the interplay of language and experience, navigating inner turmoil and fragmented identity throughout their respective bodies of work. And despite the profound idiosyncrasies of their poetry, both achieved during their lifetimes a level of fame unheard of for most poets, and a reach and reputation that has only continued to grow after their deaths.

But despite these similarities there are stark differences in the treatment and understanding each artist has received, differences that have to do with certain sociocultural biases and the literal circumstances of each's poetic practice. Unlike Celan, Herbeck did not set out to make his name as a poet.

Born with a debilitating cleft lip and palate that were never repaired, Herbeck developed mental health challenges in early adulthood. While working in a munitions factory in the 1940s, he reported the feeling of animals or other people invading his body, controlling his thoughts and actions. A series of psychotic breaks led to his ultimate institutionalization at the Maria Gugging Psychiatric Clinic after World War II.

In 1960, at the prompting and under the direct supervision of Gugging's Head Clinician, Dr. Leo Navratil,

Herbeck began writing poetry. Most of Herbeck's output was the result of Dr. Navratil providing the poet with a postcard-sized Bristol board and ballpoint pen and prompting him with a word, phrase, or idea to expand upon in an extemporaneously written poem. According to Navratil, Herbeck never revised his work once finished, although a handful of his poems include a crossed-out word or section.

With Herbeck's permission, Dr. Navratil published 83 of Herbeck's poems in his 1966 book *Schizophrenia and Language* (*Schizophrenie und Sprache*) under the pseudonym Herbeck had chosen for himself: Alexander. More collections followed, often selling out 10,000-copy runs as Herbeck's reputation blossomed. He appeared on television and in his later years gave readings to visitors at Gugging, including the Austrian poets Ernst Jandl and Friederike Mayröcker, as well as W.G. Sebald, who counted Herbeck among his most important influences. Sebald's account of meeting Herbeck appears in his novel *Vertigo* (*Schwindel. Gefühle*); his essays on Herbeck's poetry were included in *Campo Santo* and *The Description of Misfortune* (*Die Beschreibung des Unglücks*, collected in *Silent Catastrophes*).

Herbeck's regional popularity aside, any translation of his work into English presents challenges on numerous levels.

The German language's complex grammar, with its flexible word order and nuanced cases, enables poets to create intricate patterns of meaning and rhythm that can be difficult to replicate in English. Moreover, German poetry frequently relies on compound words (Herbeck, like Celan, takes these to their extreme) and cultural references that may not track for English-speaking readers.

Austrian German poetry introduces additional complexity, often incorporating regional dialects, idiomatic expressions, and cultural references specific to Austrian readers.

Herbeck's relationship to language presents still another consideration. A good portion of it borrows structures, rhythms, word-choice, imagery, and occasionally direct quotes from 19th Century and earlier German-language poetry. A clear instance of the latter is in Herbeck's poem "The Water" ("Das Wasser), wherein the penultimate line, "from water have we learned it" is a direct quote from Wilhelm Müller's "Das Wandern ist des Müllers Lust" ("vom Wasser haben wir's gelernt"), and which Herbeck may have first encountered via Franz Schubert's song cycle "Die schöne Müllerin."*

Just as often, Herbeck's language use defies conventional linguistic and literary structures, embracing fragmented syntax, abrupt shifts in tone, and unconventional imagery. His poems are ripe with private symbols, neologisms, and layered metaphors that hold deeply personal significance, often opaque and, indeed, likely hidden out of a sense of protection.

In a *Paris Review* interview, Sebald reported that he sought out his meeting with Herbeck to gain insight into "some of the basic conditions of creativity." Like Sebald, we have been brought by Herbeck's work to examine some fundamental questions about art, intentionality, and even epistemology—by which we mean the discourse according to which some people are categorized mentally ill. In the words of Foucault's introduction to his *History of Madness* (*Folie et Déraison: Histoire de la folie à l'âge classique*):

* The translators thank Liv Rahel Schwenk for identifying the source.

> The constitution of madness as mental illness, at the end of the eighteenth century, bears witness to a rupture in a dialogue . . . and expels from the memory all those imperfect words, of no fixed syntax, spoken falteringly, in which the exchange between madness and reason was carried out. The language of psychiatry, which is a monologue by reason about madness, could only have come into existence in such a silence. My intention was not to write a history of that language, but rather draw up the archeology of that silence.*

Herbeck's work, like the artistic production of many people who have been medically and/or juridically declared insane, exists in an uneasy zone between art and symptom. Indeed, the scholar Gregor Hens devotes a substantial article to demonstrating, through a close reading of "Christmas 1967" ("Weihnachten 1967"), that Herbeck's work is not poetry but rather a byproduct of illness. Herbeck's art is thereby dismissed as nothing more than an automatic byproduct of schizophrenia.

We, of course, believe that Herbeck is an artist, and belongs to the long genealogy of poets, like Hölderlin, Trakl, and Celan (just to speak of the German-language tradition) who wrestled with mental illness and whose work bears its mark. This does not invalidate their work by placing it beyond the canon of the rational. Rather, it makes such work heroic. In the words of Antonin Artaud, another artist who belongs to this lineage, this art carries on the task of "signaling through the flames."

---

* Foucault, Michel. 2006. *History of Madness*. Translated by Jonathan Murphy and Jean Khalfa. New York: Routledge.

Further, Herbeck's work raises the question of how we delimit sanity and insanity in an age of collective social and political derangement.

Herbeck lived through the apocalypse of Nazism, the Anschluss, and the Second World War, all of which cast their shadows in his poems and allow us to reencounter through his artistry what we thought was familiar. In one of Sebald's essays on Herbeck, "The Little Hare, Child of the Hare" ("Des Häschens Kind, der kleine Has"), he writes about Herbeck's poem "The Sword" ("Das Schwert"): "I wish all my countrymen would take it to heart."

As the US endures its own authoritarian season, in an apparent demonstration that *we have learned nothing* from the twentieth century, the work of Ernst Herbeck has been a reminder to us that the lone, frail, vulnerable, and disregarded voice can still speak prophetically. We hope that these translations may speak to you.

David Brazil and Gary Sullivan, June 2026

In His One Languages

Der Morgen

Im Herbst da reiht der
Feenwind
da sich im Schnee die
Mähnen treffen.
Amseln pfeifen heer
im Wind und fressen.

[1960]

Morning

In fall there aligns the
                    fairies-wind
as in the snow the
manes beat.
Blackbirds piping prowed
in the wind and eat.

Der Traum

Der Traum ist ein Papier
der Traum ist zur Nacht
da kam der Pförtner
der die Tore aufmacht.

der Traum ist klares Licht
Der *Tod* ist die Frau
der Der Tag ist der Traum
und der Baum ist der Traum

[date unknown, 1960–65]

The Dream

The dream is a paper
the dream is for night
when came the porter
who opens the doors.

the dream is clear light
Death is the woman
who The Day is the dream
and the tree is the dream

Der Mund.

Nicht jeder Mensch hat einen Mund
mancher Mund ist disqualifiziert
oder operiert. So wie bei mir
der Arzt sagt jeder Mensch hat
einen Mund. der Mund ist
besonders zum essen da. Der Mund
besteht aus der Oberlippe und der
Unterlippe, dem Nachen und dem
Zapferl. Den Zähnen am Oberkiefer
und auch am Unterkiefer. Die Halbe
Nase gehört auch zum Mund. Ebenso
die beiden Ohrlappen und der Zeigefin-
ger wenn man ihn in den Mund gesteckt
hat.

[May 6, 1970]

The Mouth.

Not every man has a mouth
many a mouth is disqualified
or operated. Just as with me
the doctor says every man has
a mouth. the mouth is
especially there for eating. The mouth
exists from the upper lip and the
lower lip, the sloop and the
uvula. From the teeth of the upper jaw
and also the lower jaw. Half
of the nose belongs also to the mouth. Just as
both earlobes and the pointer fin-
ger when into the mouth one has stuck
it.

Die Sprache.

a + *b* leuchten im Klee.
Blumen am Rande des Feldes.
die Sprache. –
die Sprache ist dem Tier verfallen.
und mutet im *a* des Lautes.
das *c* zischt nur so umher und
        ist auch kurz dann sein
                        Gewehr.

[March 17, 1967]

Language.

a + *b* glister in clover.
Flowers at the edge of the field.
language. –
language is fallen to the beast.
and douses in the *a* of sound.
the *c* hisses only so around and
    is also briefly its
        rifle.

Die Poesie

Die Poesie ist eine mündliche Form der Prägung der Geschichte in Zeitlupe. Die Poesie ist eine Dichtung. Der Lehrer hat uns in der Schule gelehrt, daß Poesie eine Dichtung ist. Die Poesie ist auch eine Abneigung zur Wirklichkeit die schwerer ist als diese. Die Poesie ist eine Übertragung der Obrigkeit zum Schüler. Der Schüler lernt die Poesie und das ist die Geschichte im Buche. Die Poesie lernt man vom Tiere aus, das sich im Wald befindet. Berühmte Geschichteschreiber sind die Gazellen.

[March 1970]

Poetry

Poetry is an oral form of minting history in slow motion. Poetry is a poem. The teacher taught us in school that poetry is a poem. Poetry is also an aversion to reality heavier than this. Poetry is a transmission of authority to the pupil. The pupil learns poetry, and that is the history in the book. One learns poetry from beasts one finds in the woods. Famous historians are the gazelles.

Das Gesicht

Das Gesicht ist manchesmal rund
und länglich. –
Die Augen als die Treue gilt.
die Nase in der Mitte ist.
der Mund. Das Gesicht.
die Menschen und Jeder hat ein
Gesicht.
Das Gesicht is der erste Blickfänger
der Menschen.

[October 23, 1963]

The Face

The face is sometimes round
and longish. –
The eyes count loyalty as.
the nose in the middle is.
the mouth. The face.
men and everyone hath a
face.
The face is the first eyecatcher
of men.

Die Maske

Die Maske ist Lieb, ach wenn sie mir nur blieb
Die Maske ist rund Die Maske Ist rund, Die
Maske ist rot Die Maske ist echt
Die Maske ist Sehr schön. Die Maske dient zum auf-
setzen. Die Maske sie ist auch dicht
Die Maske dient für einen Ball Die Maske Blieb ihm.

[date unknown, 1960–65]

The Mask

The mask is love, oh if only it stayed with me
The mask is round The Mask Is round, The
Mask is red The Mask is real
The Mask is Real nice. The mask serves to put
on. The mask is also thick
The mask works for a ball The Mask Stays for it.

Der Patient

die Katze ist ein Lamm des Friedens.
so denkte ein Dichter seiner Zeit.
die im inneren Zeichen eines Psychiaters
einer eigenen Welt gehorcht, – dem Patienten.
der Arzt zieht die Nummer dann
dem Patienten eine neue Seele an.
der im neuen Geiste einer Krankheit,
immer weiterziehen soll.

[April 19, 1967]

The Patient

the cat is a lamb of peace.
so thunk a poet of his time.
which in the inner signs of a psychiatrist
heeds its own world, – the patient.
the doctor dresses the number then
the patient a new soul.
who in the new spirit of an illness
always must move on.

Der Psychiater.

Der Psychiater ist der Sorge des
Patienten.
Der Psychiater dankt und denkt über
den Patienten.
Der Psychiater denkt und schützt die
Worte des Patienten.

[April 19, 1967]

The Psychiatrist.

The psychiatrist is the care of the
patient.
The psychiatrist thanks and thinks about
the patient.
The psychiatrist thinks and shelters the
words of the patient.

Patient und Dichter

Je größer das Leid
desto kleiner der Dichter

Umso härter die Arbeit
Umso tiefer der Sinn

Je größer das Unheil
desto härter der Kampf

Umso ärger der Verlust
desto irrsinniger die Verdammten.

[December 22, 1967]

Patient and Poet

The greater the hurt
the smaller the poet

The harder the labor
The deeper the sense

The greater the mishap
the harder the struggle

The madder the loss
the crazier the damned.

Der Psychiater.

Der Psychiater ist der Mann
der was dies kann
dem Patienten zu dienen
dem Arzt zu heilen
sowie der Sorge der Anstalt zu helfen
den neuen Geist eines Patienten schmieden.
die Mutter der Psychiatrie,
dem Vorsitz einer erkrankten Seele,
die wieder gesund werden muß.

[April 19, 1967]

The Psychiatrist.

The psychiatrist is the man
who what this can
the patient to serve
the physician to cure
as well as to help the care of the asylum
to forge the new spirit of a patient.
Mother of Psychiatry,
chairman of a sickened psyche,
which must again become well.

Patient und Dichter!

Der = Mann bricht loh sein treues Herz.
    Der Patient verdirbt in Ihm! –
Der Tod bricht ein; vorrüber alle Ehr!
Halunkenschuft, Du Hund verdirb.
                    und stirb!!!
                        Z.

[October 2, 1970]

Patient and Poet!

The = man breaks blazing his faithful heart.
  The patient perishes in him! —
Death breaks in; honor's all over!
Ratscumbag, you mongrel, putrify.
          and die!!!
            Z.

Ich.

Das Gebet der Stunde ist gekommen.
»ich« heißt das stumme Wort. Ich
sollte zum erschießen gehn und ist
in Zukunft unser Hort.
Vorüber ist das Wehgeschrei. Für ich so
gern geschehen. Nur Dumme geben
sich dann frei und wollen nun schon
gehen.
Freiheit das Wort im lauten Klang.
liegt als Parole für die Leut', –
bereit uns zu verbannen.
»Ich«, brecht, das Banner für den Staat.
die Kirchenglocken läuten.
Sie wissen selber was es tat. Um ja
nicht zu streiten.

[March 17, 1967]

J.

The prayer of the hour is come.
"*I*" is called the dumb word. I
should go to get shot dead and is
in the future our hold.
Over is this cry of woe. For I so
"you're welcome." Only dummies give
themselves and want to leave
already.
Freedom the word in ringing sound.
lies as proverb for the peeps, —
ready to banish us.
"*I*," breaks, the banner for the state.
the church-bells toll.
They know themselves what it did. So as
not to quarrel.

Ich – Du

Meine lieben LAndsleute.
Ir braucht keine Axt mehr
                    heben.
Das Land verreckt *und Du*.

[October 2, 1970]

I – You

My beloved COuntrymen.
Yr axes need lift no
                    more.
The country craps out *and you.*

Mein Name

Mein Name ist gegebenen Sinnes
                der Stolz, sein Angebot.
Er ist das Ziel und Anfang bloss.
wie er geschaffen in Aug' und Ohr

[date unknown, 1960–65]

My Name

My name is given from the sense
          of pride, its offer.
It is the end and beginning only.
as it formed in eye and ear

Ernestus Herbeck.

Ernst ist zu kurz des Namens
willen –
Ernestus paßt in dieser Sache
und etwas tiefer ist der Grund

[May 6, 1965]

Ernestus Herbeck.

Ernst is too short for the sake of
the Name—
Ernestus fits in this case
and somewhat deeper are the grounds

Adolf.

ist ein Werwolfname Name, und
heißt ERNYst HITL'ER und will
machen das er fortkommt weil
er keine Freude Hat am Dasein
und immer nicht eingesperrt
bleiben will. Sein Name richtig ist
Amadeus Mayer. er Trinkt mehr
und ißt mehr weil er Appetit hat.
er will das gericht verlassen fort
und wandern in die Stadt.

[April 9, 1968]

Adolf.

is a Werewolfname Name, and
is called ERNIEst HITL'ER and wants
to make that he gets away because
he Has no joy in being
and wants always to stay
not locked up. His name really is
Amadeus Mayer. he Drinks more
and eats more because he has an appetite.
he wants to desert the court
and wander in the city.

Mein Vater!!!!!

Mein Vater war ein begeisterter
Sportler; ein Fußballer und ein
Gewichtheber. Er hat als Soldat
unter Kaiser Franz Josef gedient.
Er hat alle Tapherkeitsauszeichn-
ungen erhalten und den ersten
Weltkrieg mitgemacht; wurde
im Jahre eintausendneunhundert-
undfünfzehn verwundet und
wurde in das allgemeine Kranken-
haus eingeliefert. September war.
es, wieder entlassen, ein Monat:
lang ... –

[August 23, 1974]

My Father!!!!!

My father was a spirited
sportsman; a footballer and a
weightlifter. He served as a
soldier under Kaiser Franz Josef.
He received every medal for brave-
ry and fought in the First World War;
was wounded in the year one-thousand-
nine-hundred-and-fifteen and
was admitted to the general hos-
pital. September it.
was, just released, a month:
long ... –

Meine Mutter.

Mutter, meine Mutter wurde in
Siebenbürgen geboren, ist eine
Russin und heirate einen Deutschen,
Bayern namens Chronas-Herbeck
Adolf Sigmund. Sie erlernte die
Näherei Handwerk in der Inneren
Stadt Wien und gebar ein Mäderl
namens Hertha 1923 und einen Jungen
namens Ernst. 1920. –'–.–'
Meine Mutter hörte auf den Namen
Steffi. Stefanie. Sie hatte im ersten
Weltkrieg als Schwester gedient und
brach wegen schwerer Arbeit an den
Nerven zusammen.

[August 23, 1974]

My Mother.

Mother, my mother was born in
Transylvania, is a
Russian and married a German,
Bavarian named Chronas-Herbeck
Adolf Sigmund. She learned the
needle trade in Vienna's Innere
Stadt and gave birth to a girl
named Hertha 1923 and a boy
named Ernst. 1920. –'–.–'
My mother answered to the name
Steffi. Stefanie. She had served
as a nurse in the First World War and
hard work gave her a total
nervous breakdown.

Das Mütterliche

Die Liebe zur Natur ist das Mütterliche.
Die Natur ist die Liebe zur Mutter.
Du sollst selber sein so sagt die Natur
Der Regen ist die Traufe zur Natur.

[June 6, 1967]

Motherly

Love of nature is motherly.
Nature is the love of mother.
You should be yourself, so says nature
For nature, the frying pan is the fire.

Die Männer.

Die Männer haben ein starkes Herz.
Sie fahren in der Gesellschaft. Sie
Führen sich selbst. Die Männer ver-
lieben sich schwerst. Sie weisen das
Leben ab. Sie haben auch einen starken
Bart. Die Männer sind müde. Sie ras-
ieren sich lieber mit einem
Philishave 3m. Die Männer haben
keinen Feind.

[April 23, 1970]

Men.

Men have a stout heart.
They go in company. They
Lead themselves. Men fall
in love the hardest. They put
life off. They also have a stout
beard. Men are tired. They'd ra-
ther shave themselves with a
Philishave 3M. Men have
no enemy.

Die Frauen.

Die Frauen, die sind hübsch. Die
Frauen haben gute Ohren, und
sehen sehr gut. Die Frauen sind nicht
so dumm. Die Frauen ärgern sich.
Die Frauen freuen sich über
eine jede Kleinigkeit. Sie haben
mehr Charme. Und sie giften sich
auch mehr als die Männer.
Die Frauen überstürzen sich nicht,
sie arbeiten.

[April 24, 1970]

Women.

Women, they're pretty. Women
have good ears, and
see very well. Women aren't
so stupid. Women are annoyed.
Women gladden at
each and every trifle. They have
more charm. And they're nasty,
also more so than men.
Women don't rush themselves,
they work.

Mann und Frau

Ehe man die Ehe spann wo auch ein Kerl war.
die Frau. wo auch die Frau zu Hause war.
Der Mann im Kinde und der Mann war.
Die Ehe und die Frau. Die Ehe von Mann
und Frau war gut. Die Ehe eine gute war.
Die Frau verlog sich nicht weil
auch der Mann zu Hause war. Die Ehefrau
war auch nicht blind. Die Ehe des Mannes
aber auch die Frau ein gutes Blatt.

[date unknown, 1960–65]

Man and Wife

Married one the marriage spun where also a dude was.
the wife. where also the wife was at home.
The man was in the children and the man.
The marriage and the wife. The marriage of man
and wife was good. The marriage was a good one.
The wife did not lie because
the man was also at home. The housewife
was also not blind. The marriage of the man
but also the wife a good hand.

Die Braut

Die Braut war laute einzig dar wo auch
im Spital die Schönheit war auch die Braut
am Atelar. Wo Rauch und mancher Arme
ist. Die Braut und kehr ein Mist war
und ihn wegzukehren dar. Die Braut
war auch hier an der bar. Die Braut
schlal oft vorsich hin und labsalin sie
lehnte auch. wo auch die Braut ein
kleines Wettchen war.

[date unknown, 1960–65]

The Bride

The bride was was loud only there where also
in the hospital beauty was also the bride
at the atelar. Where smoke and many a poor one
is. The bride was and sweeps a dungheap
and swept him away there. The bride
was also here in the bar. The bride
milg often before herself and enlivenin she
leaned also. Where also the bride was
a li'l wagerette.

Die Frau In Mir.

Hoch droben auf dem Berg
Wo die Zwei Englein stehn.
Dort ist dann auch noch – ein Zwerg
Er soll die Wache sehn.
Immer grün auf diesen Höhn.
Dort in dem dunklen Wald
Dort habe ich ganz schön.
Das Wörtlein Frau gelallt.

[October 5, 1968]

The Woman In Me.

High up there on the peak
Where the two cherubs stand.
There is then even still—a dwarf
He should observe the watch.
Always green at these heights.
There in the dark wood
There I had it very good.
The wordling woman slurred.

Der Mannmensch

Wenn Menschen. Die Menschen sehen.
Und am Auenwelt vergehen. Menschen
Wilde kommen Menschen sehen.
                                        und vergehen.
Wenn Menschen kommen mögen.
                Sie auch sprechen und dich sehen.

[date unknown, 1960–65]

The Manhuman

When humans. The humans see.
And pass in the wetworld. Humans
savage humans come see.
                    them pass away.
When humans want to come
   They also speak and see you.

Der Zwergck

Wo im tiefen Wald der Zwerg auch ist.
Da hohl ich meine Frau und ißt sein mal
au, der Wald hinab geht tief zur Sein
da hör ich meine Stimme wieder der
Zwerg im
Wald.

[date unknown, 1960–65]

Elfesteem

Where in the deep wood the dwarf also is.
There hollow I my woman and eats his mealtime
oh, the wood goes down deep into Being
there I hear my voice again the
                                        dwarf in the
                                        wood.

Die Höhle

Als Felsen rund die Höhle war.
Da stand der Bär davor
das Lied ein Brombär und sang.
was soll ich mit ihm machen?
Als mich er sah so freundlich auf uns!
Der große Tag war für mich da.
Die Höhle in Virginia.
Da hörte das Brummen auf und ein
Lied erklang.

[date unknown, 1960–65]

The Cave

When rock round the cave was.
There stood the bear before it
the song a bramblebear and sang.
What should I do with him?
As he looked to me so kindly to us!
That there was the big day for me.
The cave in Virginia.
There the growl desisted and a
song rang out.

Die Schlange

Als ich sie sah da stand ich vor ihr.
weiß wie der Schnee.
Als ich davor war da stand ich auf
                                        auf einmal auf.
Als sie schön war sah sie ganz anders aus.
Lang wie der schopf war sein Rumpf.
aus im noch etwas zu machen.
sehr schwer zu sehen den ich war dein.

[date unknown, 1960–65]

The Serpent

When I saw her there I stood before her.
white as the snow.
When I was before here there I got up
at once up.
When she was lovely she seemed all different.
Long as the curls was her trunk.
out in the still something to do.
very hard to see for I was yours.

Der Drache

Baum die Bäume in der Au
darin der Drache mit sein Mann
Hoch in der Luft das Mannschaftsschild
aus Papier der Drache.
stand er auf und gab ihm die Hand
aus vierkant Summe gelaut. –
aus Wissen und Durst der Drache mit
seinem Maul.

[date unknown, 1960–65]

The Dragon

Tree the trees in the floodplain
therein the dragon with its man
High in the air the team's shield
the dragon from paper.
he stood up and gave it his hand
from square sum sounded. —
from knowledge and thirst the dragon with
his maw.

Das Schwert

Dir liebes Heij heliges Schwert.
mit willen tief geprangert ist.
mit dem alten Testament.
panzte sich das Schwert heran.
nein leider weiter geht es nicht.
als bis zu mir herein.

[date unknown, 1960–65]

The Sword

To you dear Heij holy sword.
on purpose is deeply denounced.
with the old Testament.
the sword armored itself forward.
no alas it goes no farther.
as till to me herein.

Die Gespaltenheit.

Die Gespaltenheit ist Arbeit der Ärzte.
Diese wird auf den Nenner gebracht
die Gespaltenheit ist eine Operation.
Und die Kinder wissen es schon.

[June 9, 1967]

The Schism.

The schism is the doctor's work.
This is brought to the lowest below it
the schism is an operation.
And don't the kids well know it.

Die Sünde

Die Sünde wird verfolgt.
Der Pfarrer ist das Heil.
Die Christen und Herz Jesus.
Die Kommunion vereint

[May 21, 1967]

Sin

Sin is hunted down.
The priest is salvation.
The Christians and Heart of Jesus.
Communion atones

Das Kreuz

Das Kreuz ist rot. In Bronze.
Das Kreuz ist rot in der Sonne.
Ich bin rot im Gesicht.
Das Kreuz ist rot. Das Kreuz ist schön.
ich bin schön meine ich; meine Sorge.
Das christliche Kreuz ist bronze.
Das Kreuz wird hellobarde genannt.
Das Kreuz der Menschen ist rot.

[date unknown, 1960–65]

The Cross

The cross is red. In bronze.
The cross is red in the sun.
I am red in the face.
The cross is red. The cross is lovely.
i am lovely I think; my worry.
The cross of Christ is bronze.
The cross is called halberd.
The cross of mankind is red.

Das Feuer

Heida das Feuer ein heiliger
                    Strauch.
ein Heller und ein Batzen.
Ein Rauch der Flieder wächst.
Am Hause roter Hahn einssteht.
das Heute noch vor kurzem
Ein Haus gewesen ist.

[date unknown, 1960–65]

Fire

Heida the fire a holy
                    bush.
a penny and a dime.
A smoke from lilac waxes.
At the house the red rooster answers for.
that even today or recently
Has been a house.

Die Luft

Dick überm Horizont
da weht die Luft.
weht auch an dir vorbei
weil ein außer die Luft gewesen ist.
mindest reine Luft wird nicht gesehen.
andere Luft ist auch kaum zu sehen.
Da am Hause keine Luft ist
ist sie überm Dache fast vier Meter
hoch.

[date unknown, 1960–65]

The Air

Thick over the horizon
there blows the air.
blows also on past you
because the air has been an unless.
minimal pure air will not be seen.
other air is hard to see.
since at the house there is no air
it is over the roof almost four meters
high.

Das Wasser

Hell am Ufer da steht das Wasser.
nur am Bache da steht die Erde.
nur wenn die Furcht is groß
da muß das Wasser rauschen.
der Schöne Busch
schreibt ein Gedicht.
vom Wasser haben wirs gelernt.
das Wasser fließt am Bache.

[date unknown, 1960–65]

The Water

Bright at the bank there stands the water.
just at the brook there stands the earth.
just when the fear is great
there must the water rush.
the Beautiful Bush
writes a poem.
from water have we learned it.
the water flows in the brook.

Der Regenbogen

Der Regenbogen hat fünf Farben.
Der Regenbogen ist rund oval
Der Regenbogen besitzt die Farbe
gelb, rot, grün
Der Regenbogen hat auch blau und
violett.
Der Regenbogen dauert fünfund-
zwanzig Minuten

[date unknown, 1960–65]

The Rainbow

The rainbow has five colors.
The rainbow is round oval
The rainbow possesses the colors
yellow, red, green
The rainbow also has blue and
violet.
The rainbow lasts twenty-
five minutes

Die Uhr

Sehr Schön sieht man auf die Uhr.
  Sie besteht aus mehreren Teilen.
  Sie besteht aus mehreren Teilen.
  Sie besteht aus mehreren Teilen.
  aus dem Ziffernblatt
  Schön Titelblatt und aus dem Uhrwerk,
  Schön sieht man auf die Uhr.

[date unknown, 1960–65]

The Clock

So lovely one looks at the clock.
It exists from multiple parts.
It exists from multiple parts.
It exists from multiple parts.
from the clockface
Lovely frontispiece and from the clockwork,
Lovely one looks at the clock.

Die Vergangenheit.

die Vergangenheit ist klar vorbei
Vorüber diese Zeit *der Ewigkeit*
Und nun bist du wieder ein Osterei.

[June 3, 1967]

The Past.

the past is clearly over
Over this time *of eternity*
And now you are again an Easter egg.

Die Zukunft.

Die Zukunft ist ein Wegweiser
die Zukunft muss das besser wissen.
ohne Zukunft gibt es leider kein Leben.
In der Zukunft liegt der Tod uns zu Füssen.

[June 2, 1967]

The Future.

The future is a signpost
the future must know better.
with no future there is sadly no life.
In the future death lies at our feet.

Ewigkeit und Zeit.

Die Uhr geht langsam, wie das Wasser
                              fließt –
Die Donau ab, zum Schwarzen Meer.
Das Flugzeug schießt vorause mit Raketen.
Die Schnee fliegt lausig herab vom Gebirg.
Die Glocke schlägt vom Turm und ließt.
                    der Pfarrer seine Messe.
Die Leut' gehen hin zur Messe mit der Bitte.
Ab zu uns komme, Jesus Christus, bitte gleich.

[July 4, 1967]

Eternity and Time.

The clock ticks slowly, as the water
                                        flows—
From the Danube to the Black Sea.
The airplane shoots forward with rockets.
The snow flies ice-cold down from the mountain.
The bell beats from the tower and refrains.
                              the priest his mass.
The people go into mass with the plea.
Come down to us, Jesus Christ, quickly please.

Das Ewige Schreiben.

Die Erde, der Vulkan und das sum-
men der Bienen sind das ewige Schreiben
auch der Zugvögel. Das vibrieren der
Ameisen.

[July 9, 1971]

Eternal Writing.

The earth, the volcano and the mur-
mur of bees are eternal writing
also wandering birds. The trembling of
ants.

Das Leben

Das Leben ist schön
schon so schön als das Leben.
Das Leben ist sehr schön
das lernen wir; das Leben;
Das Leben ist sehr schön.
Wie schön ist das Leben.
Es fangt schön an das Leben.
So (schön) schwer ist das es auch.

[date unknown, 1960–65]

Life

Life is good
surely as good as life.
Life is very good
we learn this; life;
Life is really good.
Really good, life.
It begins good, life.
So (good) hard is that it also.

Das Leben

Das Leben der Hühner ist rot.
Das Beben der nächstenliebe ist rot.
Das leben ist schön.
Beben der Herzen im Leibe der Hunde.
Das Leben der Herzen ist lieb.
Das Leben macht den Himmel heer.
Das Leben möchte länger sein.
langsamer es Lebe die Liebe.
langsames Leben ist lang.

[date unknown, 1960–65]

Life

The life of the chickens is red.
The strife of charity is red.
Life is beautiful.
Strife of the hearts in the body of dogs.
The life of the heart is dear.
Life makes the heavens here.
Life wants to be longer.
slower long Live the Love.
slow life is long.

Die Liebe

Es war ein lieber Antwortbrief
da hieß es nur ein Anfang nit
»die« Liebe – liebe ist es nicht.
Da war der Anfang nicht darauf
was fehlte im hder liebe Hauch.
Wie immer war die liebe da.
die Liebe,
Wo auch st »ein leiser Hauch«.

[date unknown, 1960–65]

Love

It was a loving reply
there was just a beginning wit
"the" love—loving it ain't.
There was the beginning not on it
was lacking in hthe loving breath.
How always the loving was there.
    love,
Where also's "a gentle breath."

Die Hoffnung

Die Anmut der Frau.
Der Wille zur Schönheit
Die Schlauheit die Hoffnung.
Die Hoffnung das Glück.
Der Schuh drückt sehr.
Die Hoffnung drückt das Herz.
Das Herz tut weh.
Dauernd ist es der Tod.
Die Schönheit zur Hoffnung.

[date unknown, 1960–65]

Hope

The charm of the woman.
The will to beauty
The shrewdness the hope.
The hope the luck.
The shoe pinches hard.
Hope pinches the heart.
The heart hurts.
It's always death.
The beauty to hope.

Der Tod

Der Tod ist ganz groß.
Der Tod ist groß
Dir Tod ist grütze.
Der Tod ist schön.
Der Tod ist auch.
Der Tod der Tiere.
Der Tod ist auch dumm.
Ich kann in den Tod gehen.
Der Tod in der Schule als Mädel.

[date unknown, 1960–65]

Death

Death's truly great.
Death's great
To you death is groats.
Death's beautiful.
Death's also.
The death of animals.
Death's also dumb.
I can go into death.
Death in the school like a schoolgirl.

Die Schule.

Die Knaben- und Mädchenschule in Port.
ist ein hohes Haus im Ort.
die Schule der Schüler allein
und sie lernen vom guten alten
Schwein.
Die Schüler sie schreiben vom Stern.
sie redden und rechnen in der Fern.
Die Schule, das Dach und auch den
Stein.
Zu gebrauchen das alles für sich allein.

[May 17, 1967]

The School.

The boys' and girls' school in Port.
is a high house athwart.
the school where students align
and learn from the good old
swine.
The students all describe the star.
they chatter and reckon afar.
The school, the roof, and also the
stone.
To use this all for themselves alone.

Goldenes ABC

Die Reihenfolge A – Z
Das Alphabet der Ordnung
Das Schloß
Die Buchreihenfolge B – Y
Die Zwischenbilanz das C

A

1. Ein schönes A
wie es einmal war
ist – gleich –
ein schöner Apfelstar
in – Wie'n (WIE N)
2. Ein schöner Filmstar
ist ein Gebet
Wie gern ich's einmal hett (in WIEN alt Zt.)
und wie schön; als es einmal waR.
3. A A A der Winter der is da.
Winter, Sommer, Herbst und Regen
B i t t e Gott – Spende mir den Apfelsegen.
A A A der Frühling der ist DA.

Golden ABC

The order A – Z
The alphabet of order
The castle
The book order B – Y
The interim balance the C

A

1. A more beautiful A
   as it once was
   is – like –
   a more beautiful applestar
   in – Vie'nna (VIE'NNA)
2. A more beautiful filmstar
   is a prayer
   How I would have liked to gett it once (in VIENNA
   ca. old)
   and how beautiful; as it once waS.
3. A A A the winter that is here.
   Winter, summer, autumn and rain
   P l e a s e God – Offer me the applegain.
   A A A the spring that is HERE.

B

B B B scheiden tut weh.
immer Untertan am Scheidewege,
das Holz gefällt in Jammertrede,
B B B scheiden tut weh.
B B B scheiden tut weh.
Holz verzagt am Hohlenwege,
das Gehölz liegt am Scheidewege,
B B B scheiden tut weh.

C

Das Hoch auf C ist wohlgemuth,
die Liebe aber gehört dem Gut.
Dreh, dreh, dreh, das ist das C
Dreh, dreh, dreh, da ist das C
Die Liebe ist allem vergangen
Hätten wir es nur eingefangen,
Dreh, Dreh, Dreh, da liegt das C

D

D D D die Mutter tut mir weh.
Jahmer Kreuz und viele Sorgen
und das Geld ist auszuborgen,
D D D die Mutter die tut weh.

B

B B B splitting up hurts bad.
always subject to the crossroads,
the wood falls in whiningodes,
B B B splitting up hurts bad.
B B B splitting up hurts bad.
Wood desponds in hollow ways,
the woods lie where you follow ways,
B B B splitting up hurts bad.

C

The high at C is sunny mood,
but love belongs unto the good.
Turn, turn, turn, that is the C
Turn, turn, turn, there is the C
Love is everything passed
Had we only held it fast,
Turn, Turn, Turn, there lies the C

D

D D D the mother does hurt me.
Lamentful cross and much bemoaned
and the money to be loaned
D D D the mother that does hurt.

E

E E E nun gibt es Eis und Schnee.
Winter der hat angefangen.
Winter der hat uns gefangen.
E E E nun gibt es Eis und Schnee.

F

Dieser Buchstabe kann nicht geschrieben
werden, weil es den nicht gibt.

G

G G G befindet sich am Weg
befindet sich am Autozeichen
weil die Männer dies begleichen.
G G G befindet sich am Steg.

H

H H H ein Gasthaus das ist da
jeder Wiener will das gerne
wenn sie stehen am Laubensterne.
H H H der Wiener der ist nah.

E

E E E now there is ice and sleet.
Winter which has now commenced.
Winter which has us now fenced.
E E E now there is ice and sleet.

F

This letter can't be written,
because it is not there.

G

G G G finds itself on the ridge
finds itself in the autoplate
because the men settle it so.
G G G finds itself on the bridge.

H

H H H a hotel that is there
every Viennese desires with ardor
standing under the star-arbor.
H H H the Viennese that is near.

I

I I I ein italienisches Vieh
dicke Tiere am Hagen
wollen stets nach Tante fragen,
I I I ein italienisches Vieh.

J

J J J nun ist der Buchstabe im Tee
unbewacht und abgesoffen
wollen stets nach Ruhm, diesen kochen
J J J nun ist der Buchstabe im Tee.

K

K K K Soldatenfrage Dare.
Immer Blut und ohne Sorgen
Must den Sohn den Eltern (borgen).
K K K Soldatenfrage KAR.

L

L L L die Lettenfrage stell,
»Willst du Blut und Andern Kille«
Abends leide nur die Pille.
L L L die Lettenfrage stell.

I

I I I an Italian cow
fat animals pent in a ring
always about auntie asking,
I I I an Italian cow.

J

J J J now the letter's in the tea
unguarded and drowned
wants always to boil these, for renown
J J J now the letter is in the tea.

K

K K K soldiers' question kiln.
Always blood and without sorrow
Must the son from the parents (borrow).
K K K soldiers' question GUN.

L

L L L the Lettish question dwells,
"You want blood and other kills"
Evening suffering's just the pill's.
L L L the Lettish question dwells.

M

M M M die Mutter ist ein Pem
Immer Lust und ohne Gnade
Kann man schier die Gelsenfrage (l ö s e n)
M M M die Mutter ist ein Pem.

N

N N N der Tischler baut ein Gstell.
Immer Mut und ohne Plage
baut er sich den Wagen barge.
N N N der Tischler baut ein »Gstell«.

O

O O O die Augen blicken so.
Mutverloren und im LASSEN
kann man sich nicht bauen lassen
O O O die Ohren blenden soo.

Qu

Qu Qu Qu die Frösche schauen in die Höh.
schauen mutverlassen arge.
um Etwas zu fressen Page?
Qu Qu Qu die Frösche schauen in die Höh.

M

M M M the mother is a Pem
always lust and without grace
Can one almost the gnat-case (s o l v e)
M M M the mother is a Pem

N

N N N the joiner builds a framing
always brave with no reproach
he builds himself a salvage coach
N N N the joiner builds a “framing.”

O

O O O the eyes glancing so.
Heart-lost and in JILT
can’t one let it be built
O O O the ears blinding soo

Qu

Qu Qu Qu the frogs look on high.
Look acutely drained of joy.
How ‘bout something to eat bellboy?
Qu Qu Qu the frogs look on high.

R

R R R die Arbeit die, die ist schwer
wutverborgen und hart die Arbeit
kann man sich nicht leisten LALLE.
R R R die Arbeit die ist schwer.

S

S S S Soldatenfrage Tess(t)
mit dem Schießen in der Lehre.
kann man sich nicht Testen – Ehre.
S S S Soldatenfrage Dess.

T

T T T die Frage Tee.
Kaffeeplantagen Ohnesorge.
knan Japan nicht verborge.
T T T das ist die Frage Tee.

U

U U U nun spielen wir blinde Kuh
Kinder lasst das Spielen gleiten.
ohne sich darum zu streiten.
U U U Nun spielen wir blinde Kuh.

R

R R R the work which, that is hard
rage-suppressed and hard the work
can one not afford BABBLE.
R R R the work which is hard.

S

S S S soldier-question tess(t)
with shooting in the theory.
can't one not test – glory.
S S S soldier-question whos.

T

T T T the question of tea.
Coffee plantations unconcerned.
cnan't Japan be undiscerned.
T T T that is the question of tea.

U

U U U now we play blind cow.
children let the playtime slide.
but do not let your wills collide.
U U U Now we play blind cow.

V

V V V diese Frau ist ein Dau
Warum, nur fragen sie den Papa.
Ob er etwas taugt für JAGA
V V V die Frau ist eine DDau.

W

W W W Le projektil
ice pune uce scrine
Mädel lasse dann die B(e)ine
W W W Le Projektil.

X

X X X die Beine sin dim Tom Mix
Kuß und Kusr   für einen Herrnen
Aber lasse Dich nicht Pennen
X X X die Beine sind im Tom Mix

Y

Y Y Y Die Blumen sind nicht hübsch
Heckenrosen und ein Stelzchen
Vogel Amsel und ein Kätzchen
Y Y Y die Blumen sind nicht hübsch.

V

V V V this frau is a Dau
Why, they only ask the papa.
Whether he's any good for JAGA
V V V the frau is a DDau.

W

W W W Le projectile
ice pune uce scrine
girl then let the l(e)gs
W W W Le projectile.

X

X X X the legs are in the Tom Mix
Kiss and kisr   for a gentlemen
But don't you let them pigpen
X X X the legs are in the Tom mix

Y

Y Y Y The flowers are not nice
Dog roses and a li'l wagtail
bird blackbird and a kitten
Y Y Y the flowers are not nice.

Z

Z Z Z Zur Kudel ist die Blach
immer hören und auch sehen
Strümpfe stopfen und nicht gehen
Z Z Z Zur NKudel ist die Blach

KÜCHE –

[May 11–18, 1968]

Z

Z Z Z To the strugel is the blah
always to hear and also show
darning stockings and not to go
Z Z Z To the nstrugel is the blah

KITCHEN –

Wie ein Kind:

Der Urlaub und die Dame
das ist ein Gleichnis »*wie ein Kind*«.
da sieht man an Händen und Beinen
wie die Kinder sind.
Der Urlaub und die Dame
da lebt ein jeder auf
da haben viele Leute sich selbst den
Urlaub gebaut.
Ich sah es an der Fähre,
die so schön traute fuhr;
da fährt man über's Wasser,
das ist wie ein Schwur

[August 2, 1967]

Like a Kid:

The leave and the lady
that is a parable "*like a kid.*"
there one sees on hands and feet
the way kids are.
The leave and the lady
there relives each one
there have many people built their
own leave.
I saw it on the ferry,
that so intimately drove;
there one ferries o'er the water,
that is like a vow

Das Auge

Das Auge ist sehr lieb und dumm.
Das Auge meinen wir.
Die Augen-Liebe und das Auge.
Das Augenlicht die Farbe auch. (Hu)
Die Augenfarbe auch das Pik.
Das Augenfarbe-Licht kann sein.
und auch das Der Augen rein.
Das Auge sieht so wie ein Psalm.

[date unknown, 1960–65]

The Eye

The eye is very dear and dumb.
The eye we mean.
The eye-love and the eye.
The eyesight the colors too. (Whew)
The eye-color also the spade.
The eye-color-light can be.
and also that pure The Eye.
The eye sees so, like a psalm.

das auge

das auge sieht fasst allüberrall hin
wo gott uns hingestellt hat
sehr schwer zu sehen den es ist zu
es siht sehr ellegant aus den es ist rund
oben die iris in der mitte das kron das pupillenloch
ist entweder weiss oder grau.
ist rund inder höhle der augenhölle der vorhang
die augen sind nur zum sehen da und der sieght
verliert das haar und das ist weiss.

[date unknown, 1960–65]

the eye

the eye sees all most everywhere
where god has placed us
very hard to see cause it is closed
it semes so ellegant for it is round
above the iris in the middle the cron the pupils-hole
is either white or gray.
is round inthe hollow the eye-hell the drape
the eyes are only there to see and who seeze
loses his hair and that is white.

Rot

Rot ist der Wein, rot sind die Nelken.
Rot ist schön. Rote Blumen und rote.
Farbe dazu ist schön.
Die rote Farbe ist rot.
Rot ist die Fahne, rot der Mohn.
Rot sind die Lippen und der Mund.
Rot sind die Wirklichkeit und der
Herbst. Rot sind manche Blaue Blätter.

[date unknown, 1960–65]

Red

Red is the wine, red are the carnations.
Red is beautiful. Red blossoms and red.
Color itself is beautiful.
The red color is red.
Red is the flag, red the poppy.
Red are the lips and the mouth.
Red are reality and
autumn. Red are many Blue Leaves.

Blau.

Die Rote Farbe.
Die Gelbe Farbe.
Die Dunkelgrüne
Der Himmel ELLENO
Der Patentender
Das Sockerl, Das Schiff.
Der Regenbogen.
Das Meer
Die Auenblätter
Das Wasser
Die Blattnarbe
Der Schlüßesl (R) »r.«
Die Schloß + Das Schloß.

[date unknown]

Blue.

The Red Color.
The Yellow Color.
The Dark-Green
The Sky ELLENO
The Patent-Ender
The Bootee, The Ship.
The Rainbow.
The Sea
The Meadow-Leaves
The Water
The Leaf-Scar
The Kesy (R) "r."
Those Lock + The Castle.

Gelb

Gelb ist der Sand der Erde.
Gelb ist die Farbe der *Ehernen* Wälder.
Gelb ist die Herzen der Blumen.
Gelb sind die Astern.
Gelb ist das Feld. das Geld.
der Franc ist gelb. – brünett.
ich *habe* einen gelben Franc gesehen.
gelb ist zum Beispiel mein Pencil.

[date unknown, 1960–65]

Yellow

Yellow is the sand of earth.
Yellow is the color of the *Iron* Forests.
Yellow is the hearts of flowers.
Yellow are the asters.
Yellow is the meadow. the money.
the franc is yellow. – brunette.
i *have* seen a yellow franc.
yellow is for example my pencil.

Lila

Die Farbe ist schön
Diese Farbe ist ein Gemisch von rot und rosa
Die Farbe ist auch Lila wenn Lila lila ist.
Lila sind so manche Wolken.
Lila ist unsere Geldbörse unser Geld.
Lila ist schon eine schöne Farbe.
Lila ist unsere Farbe der toten Fahnen.

[date unknown, 1960–65]

Purple

The color is beautiful
This color is a mixture of red and pink
The color is also purple if purple is purple.
Purple are so many clouds.
Purple is our wallet our money.
Purple is really a beautiful color.
Purple is our color of dead flags.

Grau

Die Farbe der Ehre ist sonst grau.
grau ist im Rock im Heere war.
grau gemischt mit grün.
grau war auch die Maus.
grau ist schön.
grau ist jede Uniform.
grau ist die Seide.
Die Graue Ahnung
für jeden Soldatenrock
Die graue Farbe und ein Nock.

[date unknown, 1960–65]

Gray

The color of honor is otherwise gray.
gray is in the coat in the army was.
gray mixed with green.
gray was also the mouse.
gray is beautiful.
gray is every uniform.
gray is the silk.
The Gray Premonition
for every soldiers-coat
The gray color and a yard.

Der Krieg

Der Krieg zerfetzt die Häuser
und reisst die Maueren um;
Und soll es auch mit den
Maschinen und mit den Men-
schen tun.
Der Mensch legt die Minen,
Panzer rollen vor. –
Der Mann Beherrscht die Waffen
und schiesst aus dem Rohr.

[date unknown, 1960–65]

The War

The war lacerates the houses
and tears down the walls;
And it should do so with the
machines and with the peo-
ple too.
The man lays the mines,
tanks roll forth. –
The man Commands the weapons
and shoots from the barrel.

Der Panzer

Der Panzer ist aus Stahl
Der Eisen und Stahl
Der Panzer hat viele Schrauben
Doch darf man ihnen nicht trauen.
Der Panzer fährt in Rußland aus
Doch fährt er über eine jede Maus
Doch will man in nicht trauen.
Den er hat nur an den Rädern Schrauben
Er fährt durch Schnee und Eis
für den Man der sonst nichts weis.

[March 21, 1961]

The Tank

The tank is made of steel
The iron and steel
The tank has lots of screws
But don't look to them for news.
The tank goes for a drive in Rus
But it drives over every mouse
But you don't look to it for news.
Because it's only the wheels that have screws
It drives through ice and snow
for the man who really doesn't know.

Die Maschine

Gerne möchte ich auch schreiben.
Da sie brav und bürstig steht.
»Ja da brechen wir zusammen.
wenn der – »Mensch« – die Menschen sieht«
schreiben möchte ich, dich gerne
wenn sie sehen, daß sie geht.
Dieselmaschine.

[date unknown, 1960–65]

The Engine

Really I'd also like to write.
There it stands brave and bristly.
"Yes here we're breaking down.
when the – "human" – the humans see"
I would like to write you, really
when they see that it goes.
Diesel-engine.

Der Friede.

Zeit und Raum, – das Volumen,
bilden den Frieden.
Die Menschheit auf Erden – den
Staat;
und ihre Hauptstadt bilden
den Frieden. Glockengruß der
Arbeiter auf der Kirche sind der
Friede.
Friede den Menschen auf Erden.
Der Papst sprach, es muß Friede
werden.

[April 6, 1967]

Peace.

Time and space—the volume,
build peace.
Humanity on earth—the
state;
and its capital build
peace. Bells' greeting of the
workers from the church are
peace.
Peace of man on earth.
The Pope spoke, there must be
peace.

Das Schweigen

Das Schwere ist das Schweigen
im Sommer wie im Winter.
so ist es auf der Erde
Darauf liegt Eis und Schnee

Das Alles ist recht Wichtig.
und überrascht uns sehr
Das ist nicht im Rasen-Rosen
Das sagen wir nicht mehr.

[date unknown, 1960–65]

The Silence

The burden is the silence
in summer as in winter.
so it is on the earth
Thereon lies ice and snow

All of this is pretty important.
and surprises us greatly
That's not in the lawn-roses
That say we no more.

Der Engel.

Der Engel fliegt im Himmel
Der Engel ist schön.
Der Engel hat Flügel.
Der Engel ist brav.
Der artige Engel fliegt hoch als der
Himmel.
Ist der Engel am Boden.
Der Engel hört gut singen.
Singen kann er *es* auch.
Der Engel hat es gut.

[date unknown]

The Angel.

The angel flies in heaven
The angel is beautiful.
The angel has wings.
The angel is behaved.
The courteous angel flies high as the
heavens.
Is the angel on soil.
The angel hears singing well.
He can too *sing* it.
The angel has it good.

Die Ostern.

Heil zu Ostern meine Eltern.
Komm zu mir und rück nicht ein
Must nicht immer zu den Schildern
Must nicht immer Soldatisch sein.

Ich will mehr zu den Nieren
Als später zu den Kanonieren.
Die sich später zu schön finden
Muß ich später überwinden.

[date unknown]

The Easter.

Hail to Easter parents of mine.
Don't march in and come to me
Muss not always to the signs
Muss not always soldierly be,

I want more to kidneys
than later to artilleries
Who later find themselves so plum
must I later overcome

Ostern.

Herr über der Welt, Gottes Sohn,
Ostern. –
das Osterlamm in Bildes ahn.
das Osterei du weißt es
schon.
legt ein Huhn ein ei davon.
Ostern.
Die Hirten voller Laune spielen
die Melodie Ave Maria.

[March 26, 1967]

Easter.

Lord over the world, God's son,
Easter. –
the Easter lamb in pictures forebear.
the Easter egg, you know it
well.
a hen lays an egg from that.
Easter.
The shepherds full of spirit play
the melody Ave Maria.

Frühling

Der Herr Fäller war im Wahld
und sie der Bauer war im Wald
da sah er wie im Wagen rollte
wo das Herz im Herzen Holz schlug.
tik targ wo auch ein Knorr zu
                    hören war
und hielt sie ganz wunderbar
                    ihm Frühling.
über's ganze Jahr.

[date unknown, 1960–65]

Springtime

Mr. Feller was in the whood
and she, the farmer, was in the wood
there he saw how the wagon rolled
where the heart in the heart wood beat.
tik targ where also a gnarl was to
                    be heard
and held her quite wonderfully
                    in springtime.
over the entire year.

Sommer

Dir Zur Tür zur herein und fein
war der Sonne helle schein.
War der Somset-Sonnenwende
»Stahl.«
die weinrote Schimmer der Wiener
wälle und auch dir Blätter helle
Baum. War nur einer, der hieß rot.

[date unknown, 1960–65]

Summer

To you through The Door and fine
was the sun's bright shine.
was the somset-solstice
"steel."
the wine-red shimmer of Viennese
walls and also your leaves bright
tree. Was only one, who was called red.

Herbst

Als einsamer Melder im Walde
war ein Kuckuck ruft.
der Wind saust die Äste und
siehe da, der Herbst war da.
scherz ein großer Hahnengruß
ein Hase war ein lieber Kuß.
der Alte ließ die Wimpern fallen
wo auch im Herbst die Blätter sallen.

[date unknown, 1960–65]

Autumn

As the lonesome crier in the woods
was a cuckoo calls.
the wind dashes the branches and
see there, the autumn was there.
joke a big rooster's beck
a hare was a sweet peck.
the elder let the eyelashes fall
where also in autumn the leaves shal.

Der Winter

Helmut hört zur Weihnachtszeit
Kinder alle = seid bereit =
und wollen wir auch einsam sein.
und läßt das liebe Englein rein.
so weiß wie auch die Flüglein
sind.«
ist auch der Schnee du liebes Kind.

[date unknown, 1960–65]

Winter

Helmut hears at Christmas time
children all = prepare yourselves =
and we would also be alone.
and lets the dear little angel in.
so white as the little wings also
are."
is also the snow you dear child.

Weihnachten 1967

Weiß ist der Schnee, die Liese zu forsten.
den Arzt zu genügen, und den Deutschen zu horsten.
Dann den Doktor zu fragen,
und den Deutschen zu bargen.
die Weihnacht zu wälzen,
und die Liebe zu Pelzen.
die *Kerzen zu zünden*,
und *den Baum zu entmünden*
den Soldaten im Einsatz
den Krieg zu vermindern.
den Herrschern zu helfen.
den Krieg zu versalzen
und den Menschen zu lindern.
der Fahne zu dienen
und der Mutter zu balzen
du Liebe Not,
die Welt ist nah,
gebt mir das Brot
ich bin der Bar.
Weihnacht
Königin die Welt is offen.
Kinderin die Zeit ist nah.

[December 20, 1967]

Christmas 1967

White is the snow, Liese to forest.
the doctor to suffice, and the Germans to nest.
Then the doctor to query,
and the Germans to carry.
Christmas to turn,
and the love of fur.
the *candles to ignite*
and *the tree to demight*
the soldiers in deployment
the war to diminish.
the rulers to help.
the war to spoil
and men to ease.
the flag to serve
and the mother to court
o dear Need
the world is nigh,
give me the bread
I am the bar.
Christmas
Queen the world is open.
Childrens the time is nigh.

Brief

Der Winter hat Einzug gehalten;
Der Teich ist zugefroren. Die Fische
befinden sich im Haus. Die Frauen
gehen zur Arbeit, in die Wäscherei
Es ist halb acht Uhr. In der Therapie-
Stube geht auch alles an. Der Herr
Primarius kommt seine Visite ab-
halten. Der Klauser verfertigt ein
Haus. Vor einigen Tagen hat Pat.
Alexander einen Draht-Fisch ge-
macht. Er, der Drahtfisch, steht auf einem
Drahtständer und ruht sich ab und
zu aus. Die Weihnacht ist vorüber und
und meine Eltern werden mich bald
besuchen kommen. Es ist sehr warm
in der Stube, ein jeder bastelt. Ich,
der Briefschreiber Alexander, mache jetzt
eine Raucherpause von fünf Minuten.
Das telefon klingelt. – Das radio spielt
einen Marsch. Der Opitz malt ein Bild
voller Ananas. Die Krähen fliegen in der
Luft und halten die Tageswacht.
Marxinowich, ein Jugoslawe, ist sehr
fleissig an der Hobelbank. Wogegen die
Germanen um den Ruf des Tages kämpfen.

Letter

Winter has made an entrance;
The pond is frozen over. The fish
find themselves in the house. The women
go to work in the laundry
It is half past seven. In the therapy
room everything begins. Mr.
Head Clinician comes to make his
rounds. Klauser produces a
house. A few days ago pt.
Alexander made a wire-
fish. He, the wirefish, stands on a
wire stand and rests from time
to time. Christmas is over and
and my parents will soon come
to visit me. It is very warm
in the room, each one tinkers. I,
the letter-writer Alexander, now take
a smoke-break of five minutes.
The telephone rings. — The radio plays
a march. Opitz paints a picture
full of pineapples. The crows fly in the
air and keep the day-watch.
Marxinowich, a Yugoslav, is very
industrious on the carpenter's bench.
Whereas the Teutons fight about the call of day.

Es ist halb 9 Uhr – Wir, ich und der Ossi,
gehen das Frühstück holen.
Alexander

[January 8, 1970]

It is half past eight — We, the Eastie and I,
go to fetch breakfast.
Alexander

Die Zigarette.

ist ein Monopol und muss
geraucht werden. Auf Dasssie
in Flammen aufgeht.

[April 1968]

The Cigarette.

is a monopoly and must
be smoked. So Thatit
goes up in flames.

Selbstbewußtsein

Wenn man raucht erübrigt es
sich.

[January 20, 1978]

Self-Awareness

When one smokes, it's not necessary.

Das Böse.

das »Böse« kommt vom faulen Zeitraum.
Die Tante ist böse auf mich.
der Onkel kommt spät heim.
Die Kinder sind böse.
Der Hund ist böse.
Die Hausfrau ist böse auf Dich –
Das Tor ist verschlossen.
Das Schiff ist gesunken, die Mann-
schaft ist böse.

[April 7, 1967]

Evil.

"Evil" comes from the torpid epoch.
Auntie is livid with me.
Uncle comes home late.
The children are livid.
The dog is livid.
The housewife is livid with you—
The door is locked.
The ship is sunk, the crew
   is livid.

Der Kuckuck

fliegt froh durch den Wald
der Kuckuck ruft laut Wal kuk
und der Kuckuck ruft es aus.
Kuckuck Kuckuck ruft aus dem Wald.
jodelt und findet bald hie und da
                                                            was
findet er was so macht es ihm Spaß.
tanzen und springen kuckuck Kuckuck
wird es nun bald Frühling.

[date unknown, 1960–65]

The Cuckoo

glides glad through the wood
the cuckoo calls loud whale cuc
and the cuckoo calls it out.
Cuckoo cuckoo calls from the wood.
yodels and soon finds here and there
what
he finds which makes it so fun for him.
dancing and hopping cuckoo Cuckoo
now soon it turns spring.

Das Eichkätzchen

Im Wald und auf der Heide,
da fand ich meine Freude.
Der Förster schrack zusammen,
als es auf dem Baume war, das Eichkätzchen.
Es sprang von Alles zum Ast.
und schmor zusammen. Der
Förster fror. Und sein Gewehr.
Der Förster sah wie es gerade schah
und stach im in das Fell und fiel
vom Baume wie der Schnee.
Das Eichkätzchen hatte ein semi-
Fell von braunen Zar. Das Fell war
well.
Der Fuchs sah hin und wieder und
fraß es auf. Das Essen holen. Das
Eichkätzchen war tot. Der Fuchs war
lang. wie der Förster sein Gewehr
und schoß. Er traf es nicht.

[date unknown, 1960–65]

The Squirrel

In the wood and on the heath,
there I found my joy.
The forester winced,
when it was on the tree, the squirrel.
It leapt from all to the bough.
and swelter together. The
forester froze. And his rifle.
The forester saw how it directly happed
and stabbed in into the fur and fell
from the tree like snow.
The squirrel has a semi-
fur of brown czar. The fur was
                                        wur.
The fox looked now and again and
gobbled it up. Hauled the grub. The
squirrel was dead. The fox was
long. as the forester his rifle
and shot. He hit it not.

Der Panther

Der Pol erreicht der Panther springt
Der springende Panther
Die auf mich springen
Der Panther ist schön
Wenn der Panther springt
Der Panther hat ein schönes Fell.
Der Panther hat schöne Augen.
schönere Augen als der Tiger.
Der Panther ist groß. Das größte Tier
Der Panther macht große Sprünge.

[date unknown]

The Panther

The pole reaches the panther leaps
The leaping panther
Those who leap on me
The panther is lovely
When the panther leaps
The panther has a loveable pelt.
The panther has lovesome eyes.
lovelier eyes than the tiger.
The panther is great. The greatest beast
The panther makes great leaps.

Göethe.

Göthe ist barmerzig heut
und begibt sich sich unter Leut
Er ißt im Garten und der
Lauben
und will sich etwas erlauben.
was er kann das fängt er an

[April 10, 1968]

Göethe.

Göthe is merciful today
and makes his way among the people
He eats in the garden and the
                                        arbor
and wants to permit himself something.
What he can, that's what he begins

Schiller.

Schiller Friedrich ist sein Name
und er dichtet über Auen.
wo er sich will ein Haus bauen.
Friedrich Schiller hat den König
gebeten in zu verhören.
über Ritter Degen und Gesindl.
das sich über ihn lustig macht.

[April 10, 1968]

Schiller.

Schiller Friedrich is his name
and he's a poet on a plain.
where he himself a house will raise.
Friedrich Schiller has the king
beseeched to examine.
concerning knight blade and rabble.
that all make sport of him.

Lorelei!

(Zu Heinrich Heine)

Er singt in westlicher Ferne zum Rhein
eine Jungfrau ein Lied und kämmt
mit goldenem Kamme das goldene
Haar solide damit.

[October 18, 1974]

Lorelei!

(To Heinrich Heine)

He sings in western distance to the Rhine
a maiden a song and combs
with golden comb the golden
hair solid with it.

Der Stille Ocean (f. Gerhard Roth)

Der stille Ocean
war das erste Aufgebot
das wir hatten in der Armee
leider läßt sich das nicht sagen
der Stille Ocean tut weh.
Der Stille Ocean
ist stiller, stiller als so manches
Meer.
Stiller als der größere Atlantik
Stiller als so manches Heer.

[October 12, 1981]

The Peaceful Oceanus (f. Gerhard Roth)

The peaceful oceanus
was the first contingent
that we had in the army
sadly this cannot be said
the Peaceful Oceanus does harm.
The Peaceful Oceanus
is peacefuller, peacefuller than many a
sea.
Peacefuller than the greater Atlantic
Peacefuller than many an army.

Der Nachtpapagei

(Für Friederike Mayröcker)

Der Nachtpapagei wacht zur Nacht
über die, die am Tage sich vergnügen
Er wacht sozusagen über eine Gruppe
zur Nacht. Und meistens dort wo es am
wärmsten ist. In Amerika. Brasilien.

[September 21, 1980]

The Night-Parrot

(For Friederike Mayröcker)

The night-parrot watches by night
over those who in the day enjoy themselves
He watches so to speak over a group
by night. And mostly there where it is
is warmest. In America. Brazil.

Peter Handke.

Dichter Handke wird noch mehr
Dichten wenn er trinkt. Und
Schulden macht Handke hat haare
Am Kopf und wird sich sie schneiden
lassen wollen. Der Herr Friseur ist
Herr Dr. Navratil bitte.

[April 9, 1968]

Peter Handke.

Poet Handke will compose even
more when he drinks. And
debts make Handke has hair
On his head and will want to get
it cut. The hairdresser is
Dr. Navratil please.

Ins Stammbuch.

der Tag ist auf die gut Deutsche
Eiche Tot der vergangen Heid
die Not das Blumeheit. Blume
ins Gesicht gespritzt und doch
gelumpt der Tannenhort.

[April 11, 1968]

One for the Books.

the day is on the good German
oak Dead the departed heathe
the need of flowerhood. Flower
sprayed in the face and still
ragged is the fir-tree-fort.

Mein Herz.

Mein Herz schlug bis auf den heutigen
Tag wirklich normal. Die Schrift war
kurrent. Der Zaun war hoch die Tigerin war rot.
vor Wut. Die Kaserne lag in meiner Nähe.
Das Herz schlug warm. Das blut lag
in den Adern.

[September 13, 1972]

My Heart.

My heart beat along until this day
totally normal. The writing was
cursive. The fence was high the tigress was red.
with rage. The barracks lay near me.
The heart beat warm. The blood lay
in the veins.

Das Blut.

Das Blut ist die Wahrheit.
Die Schüler müssen sich einer Blut-
probe unterziehen.
Es gibt ein A und O-Blut.
Das Blut gibt Ausdruck über den Körper-
bau.
Je schwerer der Mensch ist, desto mehr
Blut hat er.

[April 8, 1967]

The Blood.

The blood is the truth.
The students must undergo a
  blood test.
There is A and O blood.
Blood gives expression to the phys-
  ique.
The heavier the man is, the more
  blood he has.

Einige Tips für ein langes Leben.

1. Rechtzeitig heiraten.
2. Regelmäßig in die Kirche gehen.
3. Eine kleine Kinderschar bekommen.
4. Nicht viel streiten und ebensowenig trinken.
5. Vater und Mutter ehren.
6. Nicht überanstrengen, aber doch Geld verdienen.
7. Die ganze Wahrheit sagen und nicht lügen.
8. Das liebe Geld zählen, bevor man es ausgibt.
9. Nicht weinen, mehr lachen.
10. Man soll das Essen verspeisen, nicht fressen.

[January 1, 1971]

A Few Tips for a Long Life.

1. Marry punctually.
2. Go to church regularly.
3. Beget a small troop of children.
4. Don't fight much and drink just as little.
5. Honor thy father and mother.
6. Don't overwork yourself, but still make money.
7. Tell the whole truth and don't lie.
8. Count your pretty pennies before you spend them.
9. No whining, more laughing.
10. One should partake of food, not pig out.

Der Bleistift zählt die Zeilen
eurer Lieder. Die Sonne steht
am Himmelszelt.

[June 24, 1971]

THE PENCIL COUNTS the lines
of your songs. The sun stands
in the heaventent.

EUER WAHN

bitte, davon weiß ich
nichts. Herr Primar.

[October 24, 1971]

YOUR MADNESS

please, I know nothing
about it. Mr. Clinic Head.

Der Abgrund.

Lieber Herr Primar Dr. Navratil
Ich kann nicht mehr. sprechen
rundherum, weil ich diese ver-
loren habe.

[1971]

The Abyss.

Dear Mr. Clinic Head Dr. Navratil
I can no longer. speak
roundabout, for I have
lost them.

VEREHRTE ZUHÖRER WIR
senden aus Vorarlberg
um fünfzehn Uhr. Bis
auf weiteres auf Wie-
derhöhren.

[October 24, 1971]

HONORED LISTENERS WE
broadcast from Vorarlberg
at three p.m. Until
further notice until we
hear you again.

Notes on the Text

In His One Languages

The title of this book was taken from one of four English-language poems included in Gisela Steinlechner's *The Hare!!!!* (*Der Hase!!!!*). The poem in full reads:

> The Garden.
>
> High in the morning is the room.
> the garden is in the middle of
> this house.
> Her garden is the mothers one.
> use can speak in his one lang-
> uages.

Steinlechner is the sole editor of Herbeck's work to include any of his English-language poems in a collection; however, no reference is made to these four poems—or to how many other such poems Herbeck may have written—in the Forward or Afterword. These four anomalies prompted us to ask: "How might Herbeck have translated his German-language poems into English?"

Morning

"Der Morgen" was the first poem Leo Navratil prompted Herbeck to write, at some time in 1960. This poem and poems dated "[date unknown, 1960–65]" were included in Leo Navratil's *Schizophrenie und Sprache. Zur Psychologie der Dichtung*. Two subsequent Navratil-edited publications, *Alexanders poetische Texte*

(1977) and *Im Herbst da reiht der Feenwind* (1992), feature all 83 poems published in *Schizophrenie und Sprache* in their original order. Gisela Steinlechner's *Der Hase!!!!* (2020) breaks with this tradition, loosening Herbeck's work from its heavily clinical framing.

In German, "Heer" with a capital H would be "army" and "hier" would be the correct German spelling for "here." We originally landed on "afield" as a way of retaining both resonances. However, an argument can be made for a third possibility: "hehr," an older German word meaning "proud" or "sublime" often used in nature poetry. Our solution to include this third meaning into the mix is "prowed." We leave the reader to untangle how it might suggest all three.

The Dream

"Der Traum," although not Herbeck's first-written poem, appears first, followed by "Der Morgen," in every German-language collection, including Steinlechner's. This tradition seems to enforce a narrative of the dreamer awakening into the reality of the poems that follow. Sullivan broke with that tradition by reversing their usual order in *Everyone Has a Mouth* (2010) and we have retained this reordering in the present volume.

The Mouth.

"Das Zapferl" is Austrian-German for uvula.

Die Poesie

Prose and un-lineated poetry appear in all original editions fully justified; we have retained this treatment in the present edition.

I – You

Melissa Moore's version, published in *Gargoyle* in 1990, is made up of two separate poems (the above, plus an untitled poem beginning "Ein bisserl aufpassen. und ... ," written a year apart (1970, 1971, respectively). It isn't clear whether this is a mistake made by Moore or *Gargoyle*, or if it might have been an intentional, creative suture.

Motherly

The German phrase "vom Regen in die Traufe kommt" (literally, "to come from the rain to the eaves") is analogous to the English idiom "out of the frying pan and into the fire" – from a bad situation to a worse one.

Man and Wife

The initial "Ehe" posits an untranslatable pun ("Marriage"/"before") that we gestured toward using the past-tense "married."

The Woman In Me.

It is worth remembering that the experiences that led to Herbeck's diagnosis of schizophrenia initially involved feelings of having been invaded by other people or animals. With respect to this poem, it is unclear whether this prompt came "as is" from Navratil, in recognition of this aspect of Herbeck's experience, or if the title is Herbeck's own.

Elfesteem

"Der Zwergck" appears to be a portmanteau of "Der Zwerg" (dwarf) and "Der Zweck" (purpose). We speculate that "hohl" is intended to signify "hollow," but that Herbeck has omitted the customary umlaut. One could argue that Herbeck's intended meaning here was "hol," German for "get" or "fetch," but we retain our original, as Herbeck may have considered that hollowing something and fetching or getting it are related.

The Dragon

"Der Drache" is also German for "the kite" (meaning the flying toy, which is designated by an animal name in many languages, including of course English), and Herbeck drifts between both meanings in this poem.

The Schism.

The phrase "auf den Nenner gebracht" means "lowest common denominator."

Fire

"Ein Heller und ein Batzen" is a German drinking song written by Albert von Schlippenbach in 1830. It was co-opted by the Wehrmacht troops in World War II. "Heida" is part of a refrain in the song: "Heidi, heido, heida"—all three of which are modifications of the name Adelheid.

Love

We speculate that "nit" could be a portmanteau of "nicht" and "mit" (not unlike Paul Celan's coinage, in his poem "Weggebeizt" [Eroded] of the noun "das Genicht," a combination of "nicht" [not] and "Gedicht" [poem], rendered by translator John Felstiner as "the noem").

Golden ABC

This poem, written over eight days in mid-May 1968, may have had its inspiration in the children's book *Goldenes ABC-Buch. Eine alphabetische Reihenfolge ansprechender Bilder und belehrender Reime für die liebe Jugend* (Golden ABC Book. An alphabetical sequence of appealing pictures and instructive rhymes for the young), or some similar volume.

There is no quatrain for "P" in the original.

"Q" can also appear as "Qu" in children's primers, and this is how it appears in Herbeck's poem. We have therefore retained "Qu" following his usage.

Frau Dau (in the "V" stanza) is the protagonist of *Tắt đèn*, a 1937 novella by the Vietnamese author Ngô Tất Tố m, published in English as *Light Out* (Northern Illinois University Press, 2024). This book, which was made into a film in 1982, dramatizes the difficult circumstances of its main character, whose name has become proverbial in Vietnam. We do not know how Herbeck became aware of this book (if we are correct in inferring this allusion), but speculate that the novel may have circulated in East Germany and Austria and that Herbeck might have encountered it during his education or possibly by chance.

the eye

Unlike most of Herbeck's work, this poem was written on a typewriter rather than composed by hand, and appears in all lower-case.

Autumn

We speculate that the final word "sallen" is likely a misspelled "sollen" (e.g., "ought" or "should"), and have elected in our translation to render it "shal," which misspells "shall" to rhyme with "fall."

Christmas 1967

There are three versions of this poem, all composed on the same day; this is the first. Scholar, novelist, and translator Gregor Hens examines this poem in his essay "What drives Herbeck? Schizophrenia, immediacy, and the poetic process" to advance what he refers to as the "immediacy hypothesis" with respect to the language production of people diagnosed with schizophrenia.

Göethe.

Idiosyncratic spellings are common in Herbeck's work. Although these choices can be read as the result of the quality of his education or the outcome of his diagnosis, we have elected in each case to read these instances as conscious artistic decisions, and to translate accordingly.

Schiller.

The German verb "dichtet," derived ultimately from Latin *dictare*, means "to versify."

The Peaceful Ocean

The Austrian novelist Gerhard Roth wrote a novel called "Der Stille Ocean," which appeared in English as *The Calm Ocean*. This phrase is also used to designate what Anglophones refer to as the Pacific.

Acknowledgments

David would like to thank his wife, Sarah, and his children, Sam, Paul, and Ruth, for making space in family life for the work of this translation.

Gary thanks Oya Ataman, who spent many hours in the 2000s translating Herbeck's poetry with him and whose insights into what it is like for a fluent German speaker to read this remarkable body of work proved invaluable. He also thanks Ekkehard Knörer for his generous insights into the original German-language poems.

Both translators thank Henry Gifford, Roz Shayan Naimi, and Liv Rahel Schwenk, for their exceptionally thorough work and wish to acknowledge in particular the many perceptive suggestions of Liv Rahel Schwenk, whose insights helped shape the present volume. Finally, the translators are deeply indebted to Matvei Yankelevich—not only for his steadfast support of this project, but for bringing them together in the first place.

Earlier versions of some of these poems were published in *Everyone Has a Mouth* (Ugly Duckling Presse, 2012), Katherine Bogden Bayard and Matvei Yankelevich, eds., and in *Barbaric, Vast & Wild: A Gathering of Outside & Subterranean Poetry from Origins to Present: Poems for the Millennium*, Jerome Rothenberg and John Bloomberg-Rissman, eds. (Black Widow Press, 2015). The translators thank all those involved in these publications for their early support of this work.

This book is dedicated to the memory of Pierre Joris, whose lifelong engagement with the poetry of Paul Celan has been a profound inspiration to us and to countless others.

Ernst Herbeck riding the Wiener Riesenrad, a giant Ferris wheel at the entrance of the Prater amusement park in Leopoldstadt, Vienna. Film still from the 1981 documentary *Zur Besserung der Person* (For the Improvement of the Individual) by Heinz Bütler. Courtesy of the artist.

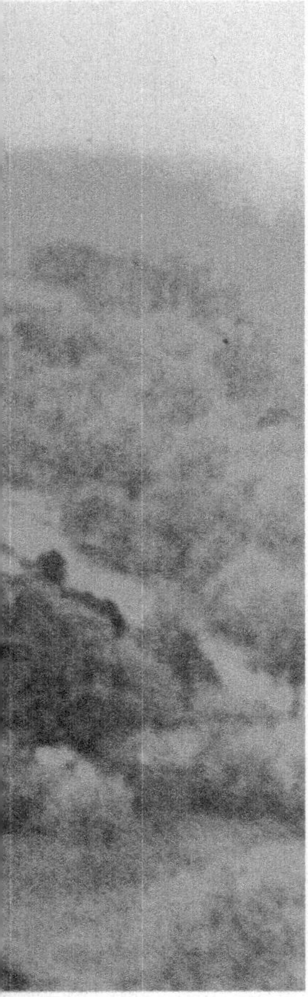

Ernst Herbeck (1920–1991) was a well-loved Austrian poet who was institutionalized at the Maria Gugging Psychiatric Institute on the outskirts of Vienna. He was encouraged to write poetry by Leo Navratil, Gugging's Head Clinician and a champion of naive art who would later establish the institute's Haus der Künstler, or Artists' House. From 1960 until Herbeck's death in 1991, Navratil prompted Herbeck to write some 1,200 poems. Navratil edited and published several books of Herbeck's poetry. In 2020, literary scholar Gisela Steinlechner edited a collected volume, *Der Hase!!!!* (The Hare!!!!), published in Austria by Jung und Jung Verlag. *In His One Languages* is the first full-length collection of Herbeck's work for English-language readers.

David Brazil is a poet, novelist, and translator. His third volume of poetry, *Holy Ghost* (City Lights), was nominated for the California Book Award. His selected translations, *profane hours*, which includes versions from German and other ancient and modern languages, was published by Free Poetry in 2023. He lives in Spain.

Gary Sullivan has published half a dozen collections of comics, essays, plays, and poetry, including *PPL in a Depot* (Roof Books) and a selection of his translations of Ernst Herbeck, the chapbook *Everyone Has a Mouth* (Ugly Duckling Presse). The coiner of "flarf" and the author of the influential movement's first poems, his poetry comic strip "The New Life" has run in *Rain Taxi Review of Books* since 1997. He hosts "Bodega Pop" on WFMU's Give the Drummer Radio.

This book is set in Henriette, designed in 2012 by Michael Hochleitner for Typejockeys, Vienna. It draws inspiration from Austrian street signage of the twentieth century. The cover, designed by Andrew Bourne at Clever Hans, is inspired by Wolfgang Neugebauer's designs for Residenz Verlag, the renowned Austrian publisher who first brought Ernst Herbeck's poetic work to public prominence. Typesetting by Don't Look Now. Printed and bound in Lithuania by BALTO Print. Manufactured by Arctic Paper in Sweden, the paper in this book meets EU Ecolabel, Forest Stewardship Council, and Cradle to Cradle certification standards.

WORLD POETRY

Samer Abu Hawwash
Ruins and Other Poems
tr. Huda J. Fakhreddine

Marie-Noëlle Agniau
The Escapades
tr. Jesse Hover Amar

Nadia Anjuman
Smoke Drifts
tr. Diana Arterian
& Marina Omar

Jean-Paul Auxeméry
Selected Poems
tr. Nathaniel Tarn

Leire Bilbao
Between Fish Scales
tr. Joana Urtasun

Boethius
The Poems from On the Consolation of Philosophy
tr. Peter Glassgold

Maria Borio
Transparencies
tr. Danielle Pieratti

Astrid Cabral
Spotlight on the Word
tr. Alexis Levitin

Jeannette L. Clariond
Goddesses of Water
tr. Samantha Schnee

Jacques Darras
John Scotus Eriugena at Laon
tr. Richard Sieburth

Mario dell'Arco
Day Lasts Forever
tr. Marc Alan Di Martino
JOSEPH TUSIANI ITALIAN TRANSLATION PRIZE

Marie de Quatrebarbes
The Vitals
tr. Aiden Farrell

Ricardo Domeneck
First Epistle to the Amphibians
tr. Chris Daniels

Dordzhi Dzhaldzhireev
Beyond Salvation
tr. Venya Gushchin

Olivia Elias
Chaos, Crossing
tr. Kareem James Abu-Zeid

Gastón Fernández
Apparent Breviary
tr. KM Cascia

Jerzy Ficowski
Everything I Don't Know
tr. Jennifer Grotz
& Piotr Sommer
PEN AWARD FOR POETRY IN TRANSLATION

Antonio Gamoneda
Book of the Cold
tr. Katherine M. Hedeen &
Víctor Rodríguez Núñez

Mireille Gansel
Soul House
tr. Joan Seliger Sidney

Óscar García Sierra
Houston, I'm the problem
tr. Carmen Yus Quintero

Phoebe Giannisi
Homerica
tr. Brian Sneeden

Zuzanna Ginczanka
On Centaurs & Other Poems
tr. Alex Braslavsky

Julien Gracq
Abounding Freedom
tr. Alice Yang

Tonino Guerra
The Honey
tr. Nathan Dunne

Ernst Herbeck
In His One Languages
tr. David Brazil &
Gary Sullivan

Karmelo C. Iribarren
You've Heard This One Before
tr. John R. Sesgo

Leeladhar Jagoori
What of the Earth Was Saved
tr. Matt Reeck

Nakedness Is My End: Poems from the Greek Anthology
tr. Edmund Keeley

Birhan Keskin
Earthly Conditions
tr. Öykü Tekten

Mohammed Khaïr-Eddine
Quasars
tr. Jake Syersak

Jazra Khaleed
The Light That Burns Us
ed. Karen Van Dyck

Judith Kiros
O
tr. Kira Josefsson

Dimitra Kotoula
The Slow Horizon That Breathes
tr. Maria Nazos

Dmitry Kuzmin
Legit Target
ed. Polina Barskova
& Kevin M. F. Platt

Maria Laina
Hers
tr. Karen Van Dyck

Maria Laina
Rose Fear
tr. Sarah McCann

Perrin Langda
A Few Microseconds on Earth
tr. Pauline Levy Valensi

Anna Malihon
Girl with a Bullet
tr. Olena Jennings

Afrizal Malna
Document Shredding Museum
tr. Daniel Owen
NATIONAL TRANSLATION AWARD

Joyce Mansour
In the Glittering Maw
tr. C. Francis Fisher

Manuel Maples Arce
Stridentist Poems
tr. KM Cascia

Vlado Martek
Pre-Poetry
ed. Branislav Jakovljević
tr. Ainsley Morse

Selma Meerbaum-Eisinger
Song of the Yellow Asters
tr. Carlie Hoffman

Ennio Moltedo
New Things
tr. Marguerite Feitlowitz

Ennio Moltedo
Night
tr. Marguerite Feitlowitz

Meret Oppenheim
The Loveliest Vowel Empties
tr. Kathleen Heil

Nicanor Parra
The Christ of Elqui Poems
tr. KM Cascia

Giovanni Pascoli
Last Dream
tr. Geoffrey Brock
RAIZISS/DE PALCHI TRANSLATION AWARD

Valentine Penrose
Of Thorn and Wing
tr. Mia X. Pérez

Gabriel Pomerand
Saint Ghetto of the Loans
tr. Michael Kasper & Bhamati Viswanathan

Liliana Ponce
Theory of the Voice and Dream
tr. Michael Martin Shea
PEN AWARD FOR POETRY IN TRANSLATION

Rainer Maria Rilke
Where the Paths Do Not Go
tr. Burton Pike

Amelia Rosselli
Document
tr. Roberta Antognini & Deborah Woodard

Elisabeth Rynell
Night Talks
tr. Rika Lesser

Waly Salomão
Border Fare
tr. Maryam Monalisa Gharavi

George Sarantaris
Abyss and Song
tr. Pria Louka

Yan Satunovsky
Prosthetics Factory
tr. Ainsley Morse & Philip Redko

George Seferis
Book of Exercises II
tr. Jennifer R. Kellogg
ELIZABETH CONSTANTINIDES MEMORIAL TRANSLATION PRIZE

Seo Jung Hak
The Cheapest France in Town
tr. Megan Sungyoon

Ahmad Shamlou
Elegies of the Earth
tr. Niloufar Talebi
HAROLD MORTON LANDON TRANSLATION AWARD

Dan Sociu
Deep Fakes
tr. Monica Cure

Edith Södergran
Modern Woman
tr. CD Eskilson

Ardengo Soffici
Simultaneities & Lyric Chemisms
tr. Olivia E. Sears

Liesl Ujvary
Good & Safe
tr. Ann Cotten & Anna-Isabella Dinwoodie

Paul Verlaine
Before Wisdom: The Early Poems
tr. Keith Waldrop & K.A. Hays

Haris Vlavianos
Renaissance
tr. Patricia Felisa Barbeito

Witold Wirpsza
Apotheosis of Music
tr. Frank L. Vigoda

Uljana Wolf
kochanie, today i bought bread
tr. Greg Nissan

Ye Lijun
My Mountain Country
tr. Fiona Sze-Lorrain

Verónica Zondek
Cold Fire
tr. Katherine Silver